Presented To:

_____

By:

_____

Date:

_____

•   •   •

Everyday Prayers
for
Everyday Cares

---

f o r   P a r e n t s

Honor Books
Tulsa, Oklahoma

Everyday Prayers for Everyday Cares for Parents
ISBN 1-56292-540-7

Copyright © 2002 by Honor Books
P.O. Box 55388
Tulsa, Oklahoma 74155

Manuscript written by Vicki Kuyper, Colorado Springs, Colorado.

INTRODUCTION

Parents lead busy lives and fill many roles. But regardless of whether they spend their days in the garden or the nursery or the boardroom, one thing is certain: their days are often filled with cares, frustrations, and responsibilities.

Everyday Prayers for Everyday Cares for Parents is designed to remind you that God is able—able to handle every problem, no matter how great, no matter how seemingly insignificant. The simple prayers and selected scriptures are meant to encourage and uplift you as they urge you to invite God into your day. And the prayers have been placed in categories so that you can find exactly what you need when you need it.

May God richly bless you as you apply these simple prayers to the cares you face each day.

If any of you lack wisdom, let him ask of God, that giveth to all men liberally, and upbraideth not; and it shall be given him.

JAMES 1:5 KJV

Contents

When

WE FEEL AFRAID . . .

God is our refuge and strength, an ever-present help in trouble.

PSALM 46:1

FATHER,

You are our Refuge.

Just parenting kids in today's world is a scary job, an overwhelming responsibility, but You've promised that we never have to do this job alone. You, the God of the universe, hold each of us in Your hand, including our kids, and You know the outcome of what's going on right now. Let us rest in Your power and in Your plan for our lives and the lives of our children. Give us the strength to do what we need to do.

Amen.

> *"Do not let your hearts be troubled and do not be afraid."*

JOHN 14:27

FATHER,

You calm our fears.

You've brought us to this point in life, and You know what lies ahead. Whatever that is, You promise to use it for our family's ultimate good. Help us rest in that assurance. Take each of these fears and help us look at them in light of You. You're so much bigger than anything that troubles our hearts. Show us how to comfort and encourage one another during this time. Teach us how to trust You more.

Amen.

The LORD is my light and my salvation—
whom shall I fear?

PSALM 27:1

FATHER,

You are all-powerful.

You created us with a word. You raised Your Son from the dead. You hold the future in Your Hands. Nothing is impossible with You. There's no circumstance or person that can separate our children or us from Your love. Then why are we so afraid, Lord? Help us open our eyes and see how mighty You truly are. Help us stop trying to control what only You have control over. Help our faith grow.

Amen.

•   •   •

When

WE FEEL ALONE . . .

May the Master pour on the love so it fills your lives and splashes over on everyone around you.

1 THESSALONIANS 3:12 THE MESSAGE

FATHER,

You build relationships.

You said it wasn't good for man to be alone, but alone is how we feel right now. We have each other, but we need a circle of support. Between work and taking care of the kids, there never seems to be enough time to build other relationships. Guide us to people who need our love as much as we need theirs, to people who will encourage us to grow in our relationship with You.

Amen.

It is good to be near God.

PSALM 73:28

FATHER,

You never leave us.

Even when we feel as though we're parenting in the dark, You remind us that it's not just us against the world—ever. You guide us through Your Word, comfort us with Your Spirit, and encourage us with Your answers to prayer. You have given us each other to balance our weaknesses and double our strengths. Take away these overwhelming feelings of helplessness. Give us a greater sense of Your presence. Be our closest Companion and Confidant.

Amen.

•   •   •

When
WE FEEL ANGRY . . .

A man reaps what he sows.

GALATIANS 6:7

FATHER,

You teach us self-control.

We felt like fairly calm, rational adults before we had kids. How could the very ones we love more than anything in this world make us more angry than we ever imagined? You know what sets each one of us off, Lord. Help us to deal with petty annoyances before they grow into anger. Help us to be examples to our kids of how to deal with disappointment, unmet expectations, and frustrations. Help us to soothe their anger with loving words and actions.

Amen.

*Parents, don't come down too hard on your
children or you'll crush their spirits.*

COLOSSIANS 3:21 THE MESSAGE

FATHER,

You are gentle.

Yet You are strong and just at the same time. You discipline Your children, but not to the point of despair. Help us to be more like You. Give us the wisdom to know when to discipline and when to overlook an offense, what is rebellion and what is simply immaturity. Teach us how to parent with Your gentle strength. Protect our children from our own mistakes, immaturity, and even rebellion. Make us worthy of Your gift of parenthood.

Amen.

As iron sharpens iron, so one man sharpens another.

PROVERBS 27:17

FATHER,

You teach us through our kids.

You use them to sharpen our characters, to smooth our rough edges, and to expose our weaknesses. Thank You for revealing these things to us, even if this process is anything but comfortable or easy. When we start feeling angry, help us to see beyond the intensity of emotion so that we may understand the "whys" behind our anger. Deal with our pride, impatience, fear, and selfishness. Help us continue to mature and remind us to never take the difficulty of the process out on our kids.

Amen.

Be doers of the word, and not hearers only.

JAMES 1:22 NKJV

FATHER,

You help us practice what we preach.

We know that we shouldn't let the sun go down on our anger. We know that we shouldn't let our anger lead us into sin. We know that we should be quick to listen, slow to speak, and slow to become angry. But that doesn't mean we always do what we know is right. Anger just feels so automatic, Lord. Things happen so quickly. Slow us down. Help us think clearly before we speak or act. Make us more like You.

Amen.

•   •   •

When

WE FEEL ANXIOUS . . .

"Give your entire attention to what God is doing right now, and don't get worked up about what may or may not happen tomorrow."

MATTHEW 6:34 THE MESSAGE

FATHER,

You give us one day at a time.

Help us live in the here and now and not get lost in the "what ifs" of tomorrow. You know our concerns. Turn them into prayers, and later even causes for praise. Show us what we should do and what we can do right now. Then, help us relax in Your loving sovereignty. Don't let us lose sight of the present. Open our eyes to how You're working. Open our hearts to the simple joys You've set before us this moment.

Amen.

God, who calls you, is faithful.

1 THESSALONIANS 5:24 NLT

FATHER,

You are faithful.

You wouldn't give us a job that's too big for us to handle—with Your help. But, we need Your help right now. Calm our anxious fears. Replace our anxiety with perspective and faith. Help us trust in Your goodness and in how very much You love our children. Bring to our minds all of the ways You've remained faithful to us in the past. You've brought us to this point; now, stand beside us as we walk beyond it.

Amen.

My God will meet all your needs according to his glorious riches in Christ Jesus.

PHILIPPIANS 4:19

FATHER,

You will provide.

You will give us what we need when we need it. Help us to sort out our needs from our wants and to find true contentment. Our expectations of our kids, and life in general, are high. Let our only expectation be that Your love for us will never change. We know You have a plan for our family, but we also know it may look different from the ones we've built in our minds. Help us to trust more fully in You.

Amen.

*Take a good look at God's wonders—they'll
take your breath away.*

PSALM 66:5 THE MESSAGE

FATHER,

You turn our eyes toward You.

You calm our anxious hearts with subtle reminders of
Your love—a vibrant sunset, a quiet moment of content-
ment, an unexpected hug from one of our kids. Give us a
close look at You now. Bless us with an assurance of Your
presence. Comfort us with the knowledge of Your grace.
Grant us peace in the midst of everything that's going on.
Help us set priorities and do what You would have us do.
Amen.

• • •

When

WE FEEL BLESSED . . .

May God give you of heaven's dew and of earth's richness.

GENESIS 27:28

FATHER,

Your blessings never end.

Every day we have new reasons to give You thanks. You surprise us, delight us, and humble us with Your answers to prayers that we haven't yet formed into words. You are the Giver of perfect gifts. Only Someone who knows us so well would know how to fill our hearts so completely. Our "thank Yous" seem so small in light of all that You've done, but You know how deep our gratitude goes.

Amen.

> *Bless the small, bless the great. Oh, let GOD*
> *enlarge your families—giving growth to you,*
> *growth to your children.*

PSALM 115:13-14 THE MESSAGE

FATHER,

You are the Source of blessing.

Everywhere we look, we see evidence of Your love. From the food in the fridge to the faces of our children, Your grace and abundant provision give us cause for thanks. But for the things we don't see, the things we can't touch with our hands—like the gifts of joy, peace, and salvation—we want to thank You now. You are the One who makes life worth living, worth celebrating. May our family bless You in a special way.

Amen.

> *Sons are a heritage from the LORD, children a reward from him.*

PSALM 127:3

FATHER,

You created our children.

You brought each one of them into being, unique in design and in his or her specific place in this world. Thank You for entrusting them to our care. Thank You for lending them to us. Thank You for the joy they bring and the love they stir to life inside both of us. Give us wisdom to know how to help them mature into who You have created them to be. Show us how to be true blessings in each of their lives.

Amen.

See if I don't open up heaven itself to you and pour out blessings beyond your wildest dreams.

MALACHI 3:10 THE MESSAGE

FATHER,

You shower us with abundance.

You fill our hearts and home with so much more than this world has to offer. Your blessings rain down on us every day of our lives. You're so consistently generous that it is easy to take all You've given us for granted. Remind us daily of how blessed we are. Show us how to express our thanks with more than just words. Let us be as generous with our kids and those around us as You've been with us.

Amen.

• • •

When

WE NEED COMFORT . . .

The eternal God is your refuge, and his ever-lasting arms are under you.

DEUTERONOMY 33:27 NLT

FATHER,

You are a gentle Healer.

Right now, please hold us close in Your everlasting arms. Don't let us go. Give us a safe place to cry, a quiet place to heal. Please give us relief from this heavy ache in our hearts. Give us the strength to do the things we need to do, even if they seem trivial in light of all that's going on. Reassure us that nothing is trivial in Your sight. Remind us that You know every detail and weep right alongside us.

Amen.

> *GOD's there, listening for all who pray, for all who pray and mean it.*

PSALM 145:18 THE MESSAGE

FATHER,

You are always listening.

You never turn a deaf ear to our cries for help, and we need Your help now. We can't face this alone. Thank You that we don't have to. We know that You're close and that You're still in control, but our hearts are filled with questions and doubts. We're desperate for Your peace and comfort. Only You can dry tears that run this deep, so we're turning to You in faith and expectation. Only You can answer our prayers.

Amen.

Let the smile of your face shine on us, LORD.

PSALM 4:6 NLT

FATHER,

You are our Comforter.

You are our Counselor, Healer, and Joy. Help us see You in the midst of all this. Let us not lose sight of Your power and promises. Restore our hope that You'll answer our prayers. Help us accept whatever those answers may be. Generation after generation, You remain faithful and loving. Thank You for Your care. Care for us now in a way that draws us closer to You. We long for a deeper sense of Your presence.

Amen.

"Don't run from suffering; embrace it."

MATTHEW 16:24 THE MESSAGE

FATHER,

You help us face our pain.

You know how much we'd like to run away from what's happening—to hide in work, food, or a mindless television show. But You give us the courage to be honest and the strength to face what's going on. We need that strength now. Give us true rest, instead of just a momentary escape from the heartache. Prevent us from being so distracted by the pain that we miss what You're trying to teach us. Use this situation to help us grow.

Amen.

•   •   •

When

WE NEED HELP COMMUNICATING . . .

Set a guard, O LORD, over my mouth; Keep watch over the door of my lips.

PSALM 141:3 NKJV

FATHER,

You guard our lips.

You know what rambles through our minds when our emotions run amuck. You know what we need to talk through as a couple, and as parents, and you also know what we need to keep to ourselves. Help us to not only communicate clearly, but also lovingly. Keep whatever isn't fit to be said aloud behind closed lips. Deal with us one on one about what remains unsaid. Give us insight into the darkest parts of our hearts. Forgive us. Cleanse us. Change us.

Amen.

Smart people know how to hold their tongue;
their grandeur is to forgive and forget.

PROVERBS 19:11 THE MESSAGE

FATHER,

You help us break longstanding habits.

Only You have the power to change the way we communicate with each other and with our kids. You know the patterns we've fallen into; some of them are the same ones we've relied on since childhood. But it's time to grow up and to stop defending ourselves long enough to close our mouths and listen. Teach us how to confront in a way that brings healing, not pain. Teach us how to be honest, yet tender and forgiving at the same time.

Amen.

It is wonderful to say the right thing at the right time!

FATHER,

You can put words in our mouths.

You can put love in our hearts. You can help us clear up misunderstandings and learn to communicate clearly and graciously. We need that help now, Lord. It's hard to see things from someone else's viewpoint. Show us how to do that with each other and with our kids. Give us words that build each other up, timely words that impart wisdom and blessings, not just our own opinions. Give us the right words at the right time.

Amen.

Irresponsible talk makes a real mess of things,
but a reliable reporter is a healing presence.

PROVERBS 13:17 THE MESSAGE

FATHER,

Your words bring healing.

Help ours do the same. Keep us from gossip, lies, and sarcasm. Don't let us rationalize these sins into "sharing," exaggeration, and joking. Keep the words of our mouths pure and positive. Even if we have to discuss something negative or difficult, teach us how to do this in a way that shows love and respect to the one we're speaking with. Help us be diligent in learning to communicate in a way that honors You.

Amen.

• • •

When

WE'RE CONFUSED . . .

Trust in the LORD with all your heart and lean not on your own understanding.

PROVERBS 3:5

FATHER,

You know what's best.

We've tried to figure things out on our own, but we can't. Nothing seems to add up. There's no clear cut answer. That makes it hard for us to decide what to do. Give us clarity. Help us to sort through all of the details, opinions, advice, and emotions and to see what Your Word has to say about what we're facing. Help us to agree on the way we should go and then to move forward with confidence.

Amen.

Your life is a journey you must travel with a deep consciousness of God.

1 PETER 1:17 THE MESSAGE

FATHER,

You guide our steps.

Where we're going seems like a mystery, but You don't leave us in the dark. You illuminate the path directly in front of us, so we can take one step at a time. Thank You that that's all You ask us to do. Show us now what that next step should be. We know You'll never lead us down a dead end. Keep us close by Your side. We never want to lose sight of You.

Amen.

Brothers, stop thinking like children. In regard to evil be infants, but in your thinking be adults.

1 CORINTHIANS 14:20

FATHER,

You help our minds mature.

You've designed our bodies to grow and mature at a fairly predictable pace. But, our minds are a whole different story. Help us grow up in our thinking. Bring maturity and wisdom out of this confusion. If our emotions are clouding the truth, reveal that to us as well. We need to come to an understanding together on this so that we will be a united parenting front. But most of all, we want to do what You want us to do.

Amen.

Listen for GOD's voice in everything you do, everywhere you go.

PROVERBS 3:6 THE MESSAGE

FATHER,

You bring clarity out of confusion.

We need to hear Your voice clearly right now. Quiet our hearts and minds so that we can listen without distraction. Please answer us in a way that we can both understand. We trust in Your timing and will wait patiently for Your answer. We don't want to move forward until we're certain that we're going the direction You want us to go. Once we know that, Lord, give us boldness and unity in acting on what we've heard.

Amen.

•   •   •

When

WE LACK CONTENTMENT . . .

"If God cares so wonderfully for flowers that are here today and gone tomorrow, won't he more surely care for you?"

MATTHEW 6:30 NLT

FATHER,

You care for our needs.

But, there's that voice in our heads that keeps asking for more. It's so easy to compare what we have—whether it's our possession, our talents, our looks, or even our own kids—with those around us. Show us how to rest with where we are right now, with who You've created us to be, and with what You've given us to do in this life. Replace our discontentment with thankfulness. Open our eyes to Your blessings.

Amen.

We fix our eyes not on what is seen, but on what is unseen. For what is seen is temporary, but what is unseen is eternal.

2 CORINTHIANS 4:18

FATHER,

You created Heaven and earth.

But, we're not in Heaven yet. Our hearts long to be there, to be home with You, to live in a place without evil or pain. But today, our feet are firmly planted on this earth. Show us how to make the most of today, using it to bring glory to You. Use our words and our actions to make our children hungry for Heaven and the joy of Your presence. Teach us how to be content, without becoming complacent.

Amen.

Better a dry crust with peace and quiet than a house full of feasting, with strife.

PROVERBS 17:1

FATHER,

You satisfy our deepest desires.

You turn our eyes away from the bright, shiny things we're drawn to in this world, and You help us focus on what's really important: You and the people You've brought into our lives. Continue to teach us what really matters. Give us joy in the absence of strife and contentment in the simplest of blessings. We don't want to covet what we don't have; we want to rejoice in what You've given us. Show us how to do that.

Amen.

• • •

When

WE FEEL DEPRESSED . . .

My soul is downcast within me; therefore I will remember you.

PSALM 42:6

FATHER,

You lift our spirits.

You've done so much for us in the past. You've forgiven us, been patient with us, blessed us with children, and helped us grow. Right now we feel so tired and depressed that we'd like to withdraw from everything. But knowing who You are and recalling all You've done for us helps us get out of bed every morning. Bring us reminders through the day of the plans You have for us that are still ahead.

Amen.

I rejoice at Your word
As one who finds great treasure.

FATHER,

Your Word refreshes us.

No matter how many times we read it, there's always something new, something we need to hear right now. But when life gets hard, it's easy to put You and Your Word on the shelf and retreat. It takes so much energy to just make it through the day. But spending time with You is energy for our spirits and minds, as well as our bodies. Renew us today with a fresh taste of You.

Amen.

Everyday Prayers for Everyday Cares for Parents • 41

The Lord is always good.

PSALM 100:5 TLB

FATHER,

You're so good to us.

Let us never lose sight of that. When we're lost in depression, everything feels so hard and heavy. It seems as though Your beauty and blessings have disappeared. We know that's a lie, but that lie seems so real right now. Reveal the truth to our blind eyes and hearts. We need Your help to break out of this cycle of sadness. Prevent our present state of mind from bringing our kids down. Heal our hearts.

Amen.

Light is shed upon the righteous and joy on the upright in heart.

PSALM 97:11

FATHER,

Your light breaks through our darkness.

Shine Your light of truth and hope on our situation right now. Lift the veil of depression from our hearts, and take away any negative thoughts that are clouding our minds. Reveal to us anything we've done that is blocking Your joy from filling our lives. Whether we need to change our lifestyle, our priorities, or just our point of view, give us insight into knowing which way to turn. Bring a smile to our faces that's genuine.

Amen.

•　　•　　•

When

WE FEEL DISCOURAGED . . .

> *Surprise us with love at daybreak; then we'll*
> *skip and dance all the day long.*

PSALM 90:14 THE MESSAGE

FATHER,

You surprise us.

You give us glimpses of joy, even in the midst of discouragement. Keep our eyes open so that we don't miss them. Help us see the baby steps of progress our kids are making, especially when it feels like they'll never learn. Reveal to us how our work and prayers have made a difference. Remind us of how far we've come and how much we've changed since we met You. Even in our discouragement, stir us to heartfelt praise.

Amen.

> *Because You have been my help, Therefore in the shadow of Your wings I will rejoice.*
>
> PSALM 63:7 NKJV

FATHER,

You sustain us.

You keep us going when parenting, and life itself, is discouraging. You help us by answering our prayers in unexpected ways. You provide words of encouragement when the path we're traveling just seems to go on and on, uphill all the way. Perhaps we're just in the shadow of Your wings, protected in a place of growth that's going to stretch our patience and faith. Please bless us with strength and hope, no matter what lies ahead.

Amen.

Be patient and stand firm, because the Lord's coming is near.

JAMES 5:8

FATHER,

You teach us perseverance.

There's probably no better way to help us grow in that area than by giving us circumstances like these, circumstances that are truly beyond our control. Thank You for using them to lead us right back to You. We know You're near, ready to help. That's why we don't hesitate to ask You for what we need. We need patience and a greater faith in You, Lord. We also long for a glimpse of hope to help overcome our discouragement.

Amen.

> *Proclaim the praises of Him who called you*
> *out of darkness into His marvelous light.*

1 PETER 2:9 NKJV

FATHER,

You turn our discouragement into praise.

You help us to not become so shortsighted that all we can see are the problems we're facing right now. You gave us the miracle of growth, for both us and our kids. We're all changing, maturing, and becoming the new creatures You've promised we are in You. Remind us that nothing lasts forever, except Your love and our relationship with You. Give us Your wisdom and perspective on how to deal with everything that's going on.

Amen.

· · ·

When

WE NEED ENDURANCE . . .

We count them blessed who endure.

JAMES 5:11 NKJV

FATHER,

You made us parents.

You know what a difficult job this is firsthand because You are a Father to us. But, You've chosen us to handle this responsibility and to face the unique challenges that each one of our children will bring our way. Give us what we need for the long haul. Show us how to be consistent in our discipline, as well as our love, no matter what happens. Help us turn to You as our Example and Source of strength every day.

Amen.

A good life gets passed on to the grandchildren.

PROVERBS 13:22 THE MESSAGE

FATHER,

You give us perspective.

Parenting comes in stages. This is a tough one for us, but You encourage us with the knowledge that even the little things we do are important. Show us the transience of our frustrations in light of our kids' future. Help us to celebrate how far we've come and to turn to You for support and guidance as we look at how far we have to go. Make us parents of integrity and faith, parents our kids can be proud of.

Amen.

> Let the hearts of those who seek the
> LORD rejoice.

FATHER,

You know what a long journey parenting is.

And, You know it doesn't end at eighteen years. But You provide rest stops for parents along the way. We need one now, Lord. We need refreshment and renewal to help keep us going. Show us how to best take a break. Help us set realistic schedules based on Your priorities. Restore the strength of our hearts by drawing us near to Your presence and opening our eyes to the many reasons we have to give You praise.

Amen.

The LORD is my strength and my song.

EXODUS 15:2

FATHER,

You keep us in shape.

Like athletes in training, our endurance and patience increase as You push us to our limits, and then just a little beyond. When we get tired, keep us from being over-whelmed by what's left of the parenting race yet ahead of us. Help us tackle one day at a time, one problem at a time. Bring trustworthy friends and mentors into our lives to counsel and encourage us. Put a song in our hearts to keep us moving forward.

Amen.

•   •   •

When

WE FEEL EXHAUSTED . . .

Praise the Lord; praise God our savior! For each day he carries us in his arms.

PSALM 68:19 NLT

FATHER,

You carry us when we grow weary.

You lift us into Your arms and place us close to Your heart. We need that safe place, that haven of rest right now. We're exhausted, and if something doesn't change, we know we'll end up discouraged and resentful as well. Show us how to get out of this rut. We're so tired we can't possibly be the parents You want us to be. Please come to our rescue. Quiet our minds and hearts, and fill us with Your peace.

Amen.

Let us not grow weary while doing good, for in due season we shall reap if we do not lose heart.

GALATIANS 6:9 NKJV

FATHER,

You keep us from losing heart.

You see the big picture that we cannot. Give us a glimpse of it now. Use it to rest our tired minds from any petty anxieties and worries that are weighing us down. Show us how to truly cast our cares on You. Then, help us hold each other accountable to take care of our own physical needs. Help us get the sleep, exercise, times of relaxation, and proper nutrition that You designed our bodies to function best with.

Amen.

My soul finds rest in God alone.

PSALM 62:1

FATHER,

Your presence is a place of rest.

The closer we get to You, the more clearly we see our true priorities and are able to balance our lives. During this crazy time, show us how to battle this exhaustion. Draw us to You in prayer, praise, and quiet meditation, as well as through reading Your Word. Show us how to find true rest by trusting You with the details of today and our concerns about tomorrow. You are our quiet spot in a busy world.

Amen.

He gives His beloved sleep.

PSALM 127:2 NKJV

FATHER,

You created sleep.

You fashioned our bodies in such a way that we have to stop and rest. Thank You for putting limits on us, even if we fight them. We know that occasional sleepless nights are a part of parenthood, but don't let us accept them as normal. When we're battling insomnia or night-time interruptions, help clear our minds and relax our bodies. Teach us how to help each other get the rest we need. Bless us with deep, peaceful sleep.

Amen.

•   •   •

When

WE FEEL LIKE WE'VE FAILED . . .

I know, my God, that you examine our hearts and rejoice when you find integrity there.

1 CHRONICLES 29:17 NLT

FATHER,

You rejoice in integrity.

Help us base our success as parents on how closely we've followed You, not on whether our children's lives turn out the way we pictured they would. Purify our hearts. Transform our minds. Change our lives. No matter how difficult it is, mold us into the parents You desire us to be. We know we'll make mistakes along the way, but help us forgive ourselves and each other as quickly and completely as You've forgiven us.

Amen.

> *"My purpose is to give life in all its fullness."*

JOHN 10:10 TLB

FATHER,

You forgive our faults.

All we need to do is come to You and confess. If we need to apologize or make things right with each other or with our kids, help us to do it without delay. Don't let things we've done in the past—things that can't be changed—crowd out the joy You have in store for us today. Help us to see ourselves not as failures, but as parents in process. Use our mistakes to increase our wisdom.

Amen.

Cultivate God-confidence.

1 CORINTHIANS 10:12 THE MESSAGE

FATHER,

You never fail us.

You are holy and perfect, flawless in character. We are not, and neither are our kids. Use our weaknesses to remind us how much we need You. Encourage us with reminders of how far You've taken us. Let us bask in the grace of Your forgiveness, coming humbly to You in repentance. Soothe the broken parts of our hearts. Then, give us the strength to boldly face another day.

Amen.

The LORD lifts the burdens of those bent beneath their loads.

PSALM 146:8 NLT

FATHER,

You gave our children wills of their own.

You know how disappointed we are with some of their actions and decisions. Show us what to do as parents. Lead us forward in prayer, discipline, and love. Help us to not carry our children's sins as our own, but show us, instead, how to offer grace, forgiveness, and guidance. Show us any areas where we need to take responsibility. We promise to act on what You reveal to us. Lighten our heavy hearts, and comfort us with Your compassion.

Amen.

•　　•　　•

When

WE NEED FAITH . . .

Stand before the Lord in awe.

PSALM 4:4 TLB

FATHER,

You are awesome.

Open our eyes to Your glory and majesty. Open our hearts to feel the wonder of Your presence. Open our minds to accept that You are beyond our understanding. Lead us humbly to a place of pure worship. Let our praise rain down on You like refreshing spring showers, giving You pleasure. Let us know You in a more personal way than we ever have before. Then, show us how to pass on this faith to our children.

Amen.

Your love is better than life.

Psalm 63:3

FATHER,

You show us love.

In the words of the Bible, in Your answers to prayer, in the comfort and guidance You've given us as parents, Your love is what we understand most about You. Give us an even clearer picture of the depth of Your love for us and our children. We trust in Your strength and power, but right now we need to trust most in Your goodness. As we wait for Your answers to prayer, our faith rests on Your loving integrity.

Amen.

Serve him with wholehearted devotion.

1 CHRONICLES 28:9

FATHER,

You ask us to act on what we know.

Help us to do that now. We're not sure what tomorrow holds, but You've promised us faith to handle whatever comes our way today. Give us the confidence we need to step out and do what needs to be done. Help that tiny mustard seed of faith inside both of us grow and spread into the lives of our children. Free our minds of lies and doubts. Give us a clear understanding of Your truth, power, and love.

Amen.

A righteous man may have many troubles,
but the LORD delivers him from them all.

FATHER,

You stretch our faith.

You allow circumstances to come into our lives that are far beyond our control and comfort zone. You teach us what trusting in You really means so that we can experience Your faithfulness firsthand. You show us the wisdom of believing in Someone we can't even see. Increase our faith now, Lord. We need the assurance of Your presence and plan. Help us rest in the loving-kindness that You've shown us in the past.

Amen.

•   •   •

When

WE NEED HELP WITH OUR FINANCES . . .

"Where your treasure is, there your heart will be also."

MATTHEW 6:21

FATHER,

You know our hearts.

You know what we treasure most in our lives. Set our hearts on the things that You treasure most, not on what we see with our eyes. It's so easy to get caught up in buying what we want and what makes us feel good, instead of using the resources You've given us with true wisdom. But we want to do that, Lord. Take hold of our budget and our hearts. Give us Your perspective on every penny we spend.

Amen.

> *"Turn both your pockets and your hearts inside out and give generously to the poor."*

LUKE 11:41 THE MESSAGE

FATHER,

Your generosity is overwhelming.

We want to follow Your example; we want to be cheerful givers. You've shown us that generosity doesn't spring from a bigger income, as much as it does from a bigger heart. Enlarge our hearts with Your love. Open our eyes to the needs that You want us to fill. Teach us what it means to give sacrificially. Purify our motives. We don't want to give out of guilt or the desire for recognition. Our money isn't truly ours, but Yours.

Amen.

The earth is the LORD's, and everything in it.

FATHER,

You hold everything in Your hands.

Our financial picture could change in the blink of an eye, for better or worse. Savings, investments, and a steady income are all false security, Lord. Help us to trust in You more than in the balance of our checkbooks. Teach us how to be truly thankful for every paycheck, every meal. Give us the wisdom and self-control we desperately need to live within the means You've provided. Satisfy us with the peace of contentment.

Amen.

Honor the LORD with your wealth.

PROVERBS 3:9

FATHER,

You deserve our honor.

We want to honor You with how we handle our finances, as well as how we parent our children. Lead us to wise counselors. Help us to hear the truth, then act on it. You've blessed us with so much, Lord. Don't let us lose sight of Your daily blessings. Give us grateful hearts. Then, strengthen our resolve and self-control to pay our debts and stick to our budget. Prevent us from comparing our lives with others.

Amen.

•   •   •

When

WE NEED TO FORGIVE OUR CHILD . . .

Never walk away from someone who deserves help; your hand is God's hand for that person.

PROVERBS 3:28 THE MESSAGE

FATHER,

You've forgiven our child.

Help us do the same. Show us how to let go of our disappointment and hurt feelings. Show us how to forgive completely. Prevent us from using this incident against our child in the future. Show us how to move forward, and help our child do the same. We need wisdom to know how to use this occurence as a teaching tool, not just a cause for punishment. Show us how to be loving and just. Soften our hearts, as well as our child's.

Amen.

For this child I prayed, and the LORD has granted me my petition which I asked of Him.

1 SAMUEL 1:27 NKJV

FATHER,

You remind us of Your blessing.

This child is a gift from You. You knew our weaknesses, as well as our child's. But somehow, You chose us for each other—to be a family; to grow together; to learn to love, accept, and forgive each other. Let our anger fade in the sight of this precious person You've placed in our home. Show us how to forgive with a love that holds our child accountable, but never demands perfection in return for our affection.

Amen.

May the Lord make your love increase and overflow for each other.

1 THESSALONIANS 3:12

FATHER,

You remind us of our frailties.

You also remind us of how much You love us in spite of them. We're no different from our child, really; we're still rebellious at heart. Battle that rebellion within each of us, and help us to mature. Then, do the same for our child. Show us what part we play in that process. Help us to love this child more every day. And when that job seems hard, or even impossible, teach us what forgiveness really means.

Amen.

A cheerful heart is good medicine.

PROVERBS 17:22

FATHER,

You keep us from becoming bitter.

We want to forgive our child. We can offer words of forgiveness, but oftentimes our hearts take longer to feel the truth of what we're saying. Give us the courage to verbally reaffirm our love for our child. Then, give us the perseverance to keep coming to You in prayer until any resentment we're holding onto has disappeared. Mend our relationship and our hearts. Help us to love our child in a way that brings about repentance and healing.

Amen.

•   •   •

When

WE NEED FORGIVENESS . . .

He has showered down upon us the richness of his grace.

EPHESIANS 1:8 TLB

FATHER,

Your grace never ends.

You forgive us again and again, even when it's hard for us to forgive ourselves, each other, or our kids. Your forgiveness isn't anything like ours. It isn't conditional or fleeting. Because of Christ, Your grace is not only free, but also eternal. Thank You for loving us in a way that never holds a grudge. Give us Your perspective of ourselves, particularly when we've blown it. Show us the hope of change and the freedom of real forgiveness.

Amen.

Create in me a clean heart, O God. Renew a right spirit within me.

PSALM 51:10 NLT

FATHER,

You forgive us completely.

We know how great a miracle that is. We want to confess what we've done before You and in front of each other. Use us to keep each other accountable, to pray for each other's areas of weakness, and to offer the same forgiveness to each other that You offer to each of us. Help us to never take for granted what Your Son went through for us. We deserve condemnation and death, but instead You've given us love and life.

Amen.

Forgive my hidden faults.

PSALM 19:12

FATHER,

You forgive what's hidden in our hearts.

You know our true motives. You know the words that never make it to our lips, but linger in our minds. You know every impure thought and unhealthy desire. Yet, You continue to love us. You don't just overlook our sins; You forgive them, every last one of them. All we need to do is come to You. That's what we want to do right now. We not only long to be forgiven, but also to grow. Teach us what repentance really means.

Amen.

Pay all your debts, except the debt of love for others. You can never finish paying that!

ROMANS 13:8 NLT

FATHER,

Your love is unconditional.

You give it freely, abundantly, and eternally. It seems impossible to believe that we could ever turn against a love that perfect and true, but You know how often we do, Lord. Yet, instead of punishment, You offer forgiveness, grace, and even more love! We owe You so much, but You don't ask for anything in return other than our love. Show us how to love like You. Help us make things right with everyone involved. Give us the strength to change.

Amen.

•   •   •

When

WE ARE SEARCHING FOR FULFILLMENT . . .

The godly walk with integrity; blessed are their children after them.

PROVERBS 20:7 NLT

FATHER,

You created us in Your image.

You made us parents. You designed us for love and good works. These are all wonderful things, so why do we feel so lost and empty? Are we caught up in comparing ourselves with others? Is there something in our lives that You want us to give up, but we keep holding onto? Are we trusting in ourselves, more than we are in You? We need Your wisdom and direction. Please set our priorities and desires in line with Yours.

Amen.

Stop and consider God's wonders.

JOB 37:14

FATHER,

Your miracles surround us.

Open our eyes to see them. We don't want to miss even one of the wonders that You've woven into this "ordinary" day. Don't let any of Your blessings pass by without our notice and heartfelt thanks. Fill us with a gratitude so deep that it takes away any sense of discontentment or insignificance. You, the almighty God of the universe, love us. We could never be "insignificant" in light of the One who loves us.

Amen.

> *You have let me experience the joys of life and the exquisite pleasures of your own eternal presence.*
>
> PSALM 16:11 TLB

FATHER,

Your presence fill us with joy.

We know You're near. Thank You for that, Lord. Help us see ourselves and our kids through Your eyes. Remind us that it's who we are, not what we do, that really matters. Make us people of integrity and purpose, parents who stand out in a crowd, because of Your love in our lives. We long for Your presence more than we desire the honor and recognition of those around us. We long for more of You. Draw us close.

Amen.

Whatever you do, work at it with all your heart, as working for the Lord, not for men.

COLOSSIANS 3:23

FATHER,

You make our work matter.

You not only use our efforts to accomplish good things in this world, but You also use our labor to shape our characters more closely to Your image. You teach us patience, servanthood, diligence, and greater reliance on You. Give us joy in the little things we do today, from paying bills to cleaning the toilet. We want to do every job with excellence, no matter how insignificant we feel that job is. Teach us how to do that.

Amen.

•   •   •

When

WE NEED GUIDANCE . . .

Is anyone crying for help? GOD is listening, ready to rescue you.

PSALM 34:17 THE MESSAGE

FATHER,

You are listening.

You hear our every prayer, even before the words are formed clearly in our own minds. You hear our moans and sighs. You know the questions that linger in our hearts. Through it all, You wait patiently for us to come to You. We're here now, Lord. We're asking for Your direction and wisdom. We know that's something that You long to provide for us. Help us to hear Your voice clearly, then to act on what we hear.

Amen.

May the LORD answer all your prayers.

FATHER,

You answer our prayers.

Open our eyes to see the answers, to know they're from You. We're not sure which way to go, but You know where every path will lead our children and us. Give us the guidance we need in this situation. Lead us down the path that will draw us closest to You. Give us patience to wait for Your timing. Then, give us the courage to be obedient, even if we can't see the outcome as clearly as You do.

Amen.

> *The wise man is glad to be instructed, but a self-sufficient fool falls flat on his face.*

PROVERBS 10:8 TLB

FATHER,

You are wise.

You're a Parent who encourages us to grow. You don't do everything for us. Instead, You encourage us to take part, to try, to mature, to succeed, and even to fail. Through it all, You teach us how to become wiser parents and more loving people. We need a generous portion of that wisdom now. Help us to act confidently on what we know, on what You've already taught us. Then, show us how to move forward in faith.

Amen.

> *Plans fail for lack of counsel, but with many advisers they succeed.*

PROVERBS 15:22

FATHER,

You lead us to wise counselors.

You use others to guide us in the way that You want us to go. Give us wisdom to know whom to ask for insight into this situation. Bless those people with a deep understanding of Your Word and Your ways. Use the unique skills and wisdom You've nurtured in their lives to bless ours. Please use the advice we get to confirm the direction we already feel in our hearts. Our success is in Your hands.

Amen.

•   •   •

When

WE NEED HEALING . . .

Heart-shattered lives ready for love don't for a moment escape God's notice.

PSALM 51:17 THE MESSAGE

FATHER,

You long to heal us.

We're Your beloved children. As parents, we know how it hurts to see our own kids in pain. In that same way, we know You hurt for us now. Thank You that our tears never go unnoticed. Knowing that makes us feel less alone. It comforts us in a way that nothing else can. But, we ask for an even deeper comfort right now. We know there are things that only You can heal, and that's what we're asking for—Your healing.

Amen.

He leads me beside the still waters. He restores my soul.

PSALM 23:2-3 NKJV

FATHER,

You relieve our pain.

Your healing goes deeper than anything a doctor or a counselor can provide. You lead us to the healing waters of Your presence. You comfort us with a peace that doesn't make sense in light of the circumstances we're going through. Fill us with that peace now. We ask that these prayers move Your healing hands to the exact place where we need them. Be our Rest and Refreshment. Be our Healer and Place of refuge.

Amen.

He who began a good work in you will carry it on to completion until the day of Christ Jesus.

PHILIPPIANS 1:6

FATHER,

You give us hope.

You've made promises that we know You'll keep. We know that what we're going through right now could never prevent the purpose of our lives from being fulfilled. Use this time, no matter how painful, to help us become the people You want us to be. Use it to slow us down and to help us get to know You better. We ask for Your healing, but most of all we ask that You use this time in the way that You know is best.

Amen.

•   •   •

When

WE NEED HOPE . . .

Let us hold unswervingly to the hope we profess, for he who promised is faithful.

HEBREWS 10:23

FATHER,

Your love holds us close.

You're a righteous and trustworthy Father who never goes back on His promises. Let us hold to that truth, finding encouragement, comfort, and hope in the fact that You never change. Be our Rock right now. We need to lean against You for strength. Be a solid Foundation when everything else seems so uncertain. Remind us of Your faithfulness in the past. Remind us of Your promises for the future. Then, help us hold tightly to the truth and You.

Amen.

May the LORD richly bless both you and your children.

FATHER,

You long to bless us.

Help us to see the blessings You're providing for us today. Help us to never regard any blessing as too small to be worth giving thanks for. Help us to find You and Your love in what's happening right now. Take our eyes off of what seems hopeless, and focus them on Your promises and goodness to us. Lead us beyond our emotions to a place of worship, a place where our hope and faith in You can grow.

Amen.

88 • *Everyday Prayers for Everyday Cares for Parents*

We live by faith, not by sight.

2 CORINTHIANS 5:7

FATHER,

You ask us to walk by faith.

But, we're so used to depending on what we see with our eyes, touch with our hands, hear with our ears, and feel with our emotions. Sometimes, following You feels like walking in the dark. We need Your light to guide us. Oftentimes, we feel lost and helpless, almost hopeless. But, we know that we can never be without hope, as long as You're by our side. Show us what walking in faith should look like in the midst of this storm.

Amen.

> *You know with all your heart and soul that not one of all the good promises the LORD your God gave you has failed.*

JOSHUA 23:14

FATHER,

You are good.

No matter how our circumstances make us feel right now, the truth remains that You love us and want only the best for us. Give us a glimpse of Your love and of the good things that You can bring out of these circumstances. That's the encouragement we long for. Give us the perseverance we need to not let our hearts give up hope. You know right where we're hurting. Comfort us and move us forward.

Amen.

•   •   •

When

IT'S TIME TO LET GO . . .

Defend and bless your chosen ones. Lead them like a shepherd and carry them forever in your arms.

PSALM 28:9 TLB

FATHER,

You're always with our children.

Even when we can't be near them, we know You are. Help us to relax in this knowledge, trusting You to guide them, protect them, and continue to bring them to maturity in You. As we're going through this time of transition, help us give our child room to make his/her own decisions. Help us give advice when asked, but know when to keep our lips closed and just pray. Please bring Godly friends and counselors into our child's life.

Amen.

To everything there is a season, A time for every purpose under heaven.

ECCLESIASTES 3:1 NKJV

FATHER,

You created the seasons.

You designed winter, spring, summer, and fall—each one with its own unique beauty and gifts. You also created different seasons of life: birth, childhood, adolescence, and adulthood. Teach us how to celebrate this new season of our child's life, as well as our own. Show us this season's unique beauty and gifts. Give us wisdom to know how to best relate to our child. Teach us how to let go with love, celebration, and peace of mind.

Amen.

•   •   •

When

WE NEED HELP WITH OUR MARRIAGE . . .

> *"Live generously and graciously toward others, the way God lives toward you."*
>

FATHER,

Your love is our example.

You know unconditional love isn't easy; look at what loving us cost You. But, the way that You love us is the way that You want us to love each other. We want to put what we know of Your love into practice, but our impatience and selfishness keep getting in the way. Forgive us and, in turn, teach us how to forgive one another. Give us the courage to confess our sins, as well as our love, to one another.

Amen.

Live in harmony with one another.

Romans 12:16

FATHER,

You've made us one.

Through Your mystery of marriage, You've joined us together in a unique way. But, we don't feel like "one" right now. Rather, we feel like two parts of a puzzle that don't fit together quite right. Give each of us insight into how we need to change. Stop us from playing the "blame game." Let our words and actions bring us closer together, not drive us further apart. Make us one again, Father, the way that You long for us to be.

Amen.

Keep your word even when it costs you.

PSALM 15:4 THE MESSAGE

FATHER,

You teach us what commitment means.

You never go back on Your promises. Help us keep ours. We promised to love each other, 'til death do us part. We promised to love in sickness and health, for richer or for poorer. Give us the courage to do exactly that. When our communication seems to be going nowhere, help us to understand the heart behind the words. Give us wisdom in how we voice our frustrations. Help our marriage to mature and grow.

Amen.

If we love one another, God lives in us and his love is made complete in us.

1 JOHN 4:12

FATHER,

You designed marriage.

You said it wasn't good for man or woman to be alone. But, it's easy to feel alone when things aren't going well between us. Fill our hearts with You. Stop us from relying on each other to fill those empty places. You alone have the power to make our marriage what You want it to be, but You can't do that without us coming to You in humility and repentance. That's how we come to You today.

Amen.

• • •

When

WE FEEL
OVERPROTECTIVE . . .

---

*Tell the next generation detail by detail the
story of God.*

PSALM 48:13 THE MESSAGE

FATHER,

You care for every generation.

You've offered protection and guidance for those
who've turned to You since the dawn of time. The stories
of Your faithfulness fill the pages of the Bible. Thank You
for passing those stories onto us and our children to help
us understand how deep Your love is for us. Please help us
to trust in that love right now. Be there for our children
when we can't. Our peace of mind rests on Your promises.

Amen.

Some trust in chariots and some in horses, but we trust in the name of the LORD our God.

PSALM 20:7

FATHER,

Your name is over all.

You've been called a wonderful Counselor, everlasting Father, Redeemer, Savior, and Friend. You are all of these things and more. Your name and character are worthy of our trust. We trust You now to take care of our children in a way that no human parent ever could. You are the only One who can offer them true protection—physically, emotionally, and spiritually. Surround them with Your angels. Guard their hearts and minds. Draw them close to You.

Amen.

•   •   •

When

WE FEEL OVERWHELMED . . .

I am overwhelmed, and you alone know the way I should turn.

PSALM 142:3 NLT

FATHER,

You're always there when we call for help.

Thank You for listening to our cries and sighs, just as readily as to our praise. You know what's happening right now. You know each and every circumstance that's making us feel lost and overwhelmed. We need Your wisdom as much, or even more, than Your comfort. Bless us with Your perspective. Guide us through the days ahead, as we hold tightly to Your presence and Your promises.

Amen.

Reverence for God adds hours to each day.

Proverbs 10:27 TLB

FATHER,

You help us make the most of today.

No matter how overwhelming the day ahead of us seems, You help us balance whatever comes our way. We need Your wisdom to make sound decisions and to set Godly priorities. We need Your perseverance to keep us from giving up. We need Your strength to give us the energy and stamina it takes to tackle all that lies before us. And, we need Your love to bring us comfort and to surprise us with joy hidden in unexpected places.

Amen.

Revive us so we can call on your name once more.

PSALM 80:18 NLT

FATHER,

You revive our spirits.

You call us to places we never thought we'd have the strength to go. You move us forward with words of encouragement. You lift our hands in praise. Please whisper words of hope to us now. Show us how to lean on each other, as well as on You, during this time. Everything seems so hard right now. Help us to carry our share of the load and to know what to put in Your more than able Hands.

Amen.

I'm feeling terrible—I couldn't feel worse! Get me on my feet again. You promised, remember?

PSALM 119:25 THE MESSAGE

FATHER,

Your love overwhelms us.

When life does the same, Your love is greater still. Hold us tightly in Your arms. Then, lead us to a quiet place where we can gain perspective. Don't let our fears make our troubles seem larger than they really are. We need You to calm our hearts enough to see things clearly. We don't want to move forward until You show us exactly where You want us to go. Please make that direction clear to us now.

Amen.

•   •   •

When

WE NEED PATIENCE . . .

Be patient, bearing with one another in love.

EPHESIANS 4:2

FATHER,

You know the outcome of our efforts.

We've had it. We're tired and cranky and feel as though all our efforts are getting nowhere at all. Only You can see where diligence, perseverance, and patience will take us. We can't see that far, Lord. Please take away our discouragement. Renew our resolve to keep doing what we know we need to do. Soothe our frayed nerves and quiet our frantic hearts. We don't want to give up, but we can't keep going the way we are now.

Amen.

He has made everything beautiful in its time.

ECCLESIASTES 3:11

FATHER,

You use time as a tool.

You use it to shape our characters and to bring our children and us to maturity, in both body and soul. Thank You for helping our patience grow through it all. It seemed so much simpler before we had children; we seemed like patient, even-tempered adults—at least most of the time. Thank You for using our children to show us what's hidden in our hearts, to bring our weaknesses into the light so that we can change.

Amen.

GOD takes the time to do everything right—everything.

ISAIAH 30:18 THE MESSAGE

FATHER,

You slow us down.

Thanks for using our kids to teach us how to take time to snuggle, to watch butterflies, and to play games. Thanks for using them to remind us that people don't always get everything right on the first try. Even through our children's stubbornness and disobedience, You're teaching us. Thanks for using our impatience as parents to expose our own selfishness. Thanks for not only helping our patience grow, but for also showing us what lies behind our lack of it.

Amen.

Let us consider how we may spur one another on toward love and good deeds.

HEBREWS 10:24

FATHER,

You want us to encourage one another.

But too often, our criticisms outweigh our encouragement. When we feel stretched to the limit, help us hold our tongues. Help us know when we've crossed the line between teaching and nagging. When others' "imperfections" begin to get on our nerves, bring our own faults to mind. Humble us so that we can better understand and extend grace to our family. Day by day, let our love grow to more resemble Your own.

Amen.

• • •

When

WE LONG FOR PEACE AND QUIET . . .

> *Be at rest once more, O my soul, for the LORD has been good to you.*
>
> PSALM 116:7

FATHER,

You are our souls' true Rest.

Help us stop right now, no matter how frantic the day has been, and offer praise to You. We want to sit at Your feet in anticipation, like our own kids with a favorite bedtime story. We want to see Your face and hear You speak words of love and hope. We draw close to You, like children to their beloved dad. For that's who You are, Lord—the One who loves us most and best.

Amen.

Be still, and know that I am God.

PSALM 46:10

FATHER,

You are God.

We believe that, but our lives don't reflect that truth right now. Everything seems loud, crazy, and out of control—not just around us, but in our hearts as well. We've lost sight of You and have tried to rule our own lives. Forgive us. Sometimes, it seems as though we'll never learn. We want to be still—right here, right now. We want a fresh look at You. Cleanse our minds and hearts with Your grace, forgiveness, and peace.

Amen.

He rested on the seventh day from all His work which He had done.

GENESIS 2:2 NKJV

FATHER,

You rested from Your work.

We need to do that too. There's always so much to get done that it seems as though there's never time to just sit down and be quiet for a moment. Help us to do that now. Help us find a peaceful spot in the middle of the chaos of this stage of life. Help us hand over everything we're carrying in our minds and hearts that rightfully belongs in Your able hands. Lead us to Your peace and rest.

Amen.

A heart at peace gives life to the body.

PROVERBS 14:30

FATHER,

You examine our hearts.

Sometimes, the craziness of our lives is just a reflection of the unrest in our hearts. Reveal to us anything we need to confess to You. Show us where we're choosing to go our own way, instead of Yours. We long to be close enough to You that the fire of Your holiness will burn away every impurity that keeps us from loving others and You. Make our hearts and lives havens of peace, no matter what the day holds.

Amen.

•   •   •

When

WE ARE PRIDEFUL . . .

As for me and my family, we will serve the Lord.

JOSHUA 24:15 TLB

FATHER,

You are the Lord of our family.

When things turn out well, remind us that we've never accomplished them on our own. You've given us every one of our talents and abilities. How You've designed our bodies and minds, whom You've chosen to be in our families, how closely we've followed You during our lives—these things all play a part in our "success" as parents and in every other area of our lives. We want to measure our success by how well we've pleased You.

Amen.

My life is an example to many, because you have been my strength and protection.

PSALM 71:7 NLT

FATHER,

You give us cause for praise.

But that praise is for You, not us. Stop us from taking the credit for miracles that You've worked in us and through us. Help us take pride in a job well done without becoming prideful. Keep us humble by continually reminding us how far we have to go before our love begins to resemble Yours. Stop us from comparing ourselves with others, especially when we just need an ego boost. Give us humble hearts.

Amen.

•   •   •

When

WE NEED HELP WITH
OUR PRIORITIES . . .

"You're blessed when you get your inside world—your mind and heart—put right. Then you can see God in the outside world."

MATTHEW 5:8 THE MESSAGE

FATHER,

You teach us balance.

You show us what's worthy of our time, talent, and treasures. You help us choose what's best over what's simply beneficial. You help us say no, even when others don't understand. You help us be flexible and spontaneous, while still accomplishing what You have for us to do today. We ask for Your wisdom now in setting Godly priorities in a practical way. Help us balance what You've set before us.

Amen.

Commit your work to the LORD, and then your plans will succeed.

PROVERBS 16:3 NLT

FATHER,

Your blessing is our beginning.

We ask for Your guidance in what lies ahead. We want to do more than a good job; we want to do a Godly one, one that reflects Your priorities. Help us see them clearly and know how to apply them to what we do. You created us to bring glory to You. We pray that's what will happen through us. Please bless our plans. We commit to doing our best, but we know our success rests with You. *Amen.*

> *"Love the Lord your God with all your passion and prayer and intelligence."*
>
> MATTHEW 22:37 THE MESSAGE

FATHER,

You know what's of eternal worth.

Help us to set our life's priorities in light of what really matters. We know our kids are worth more than any career or household chore, but we still have jobs that need to be done. Help us to accomplish the tasks we need to do today. But also, help us to be more sensitive to Your Spirit, balancing flexibility with diligence. Open our eyes to opportunities to show love to each other and our kids in a tangible way today.

Amen.

God-loyal people, living honest lives, make it much easier for their children.

PROVERBS 20:7 THE MESSAGE

FATHER,

You prioritize our inner lives.

You've shown us there's so much more to life than the size of our house or titles we hold. Others may judge the worth of our lives by what they see, but You know the value of what grows in our hearts. Show us how to invest in the lives of our children and other people in a way that matters. Help us prioritize everything we do and everything we are in light of Your love.

Amen.

•   •   •

When

WE FEEL STRESSED . . .

God is faithful.

---

1 CORINTHIANS 1:9 NKJV

FATHER,

You are our Peace.

Day to day, we never know what problems or stresses will come our way, but we do know what You'll be like. You remain faithful, loving, all-powerful, tender, and infinitely wise. Knowing we can depend on You is a constant comfort when life seems to be going haywire. You are our Touchstone of peace when everything else is in chaos. We come to You in need of the assurance of Your changeless love.

Amen.

Be our strength each day and our salvation in the time of trouble.

ISAIAH 33:2 TLB

FATHER,

You remain strong when we are weak.

We feel so on edge right now. It just seems as though the pressure never lets up. Show us how to let that pressure roll right off of us onto Your strong, calm shoulders. Prevent us from carrying anxiety around with us. Lead us to You in prayer. Show us reasons to praise You, even when the situations around us seem to be much less than praiseworthy. Help us find rest in Your strength, instead of relying on our own.

Amen.

> *Lead a quiet and peaceable life in all godliness and reverence.*
>
> 1 TIMOTHY 2:2 NKJV

FATHER,

You soothe our nerves.

You guide our lives down peaceful paths when we follow Your ways. Even when things seem to be falling apart around us, You provide a place of quiet inside us. Help us retreat to that place right now. Help us take a moment just to look at You and remember who's in control. Calm our hearts with the knowledge of Your love for our children and us. Use the peace You're nurturing inside of us to bless those around us.

Amen.

*The eyes of the LORD search the whole earth
in order to strengthen those whose hearts are
fully committed to him.*

2 CHRONICLES 16:9 NLT

FATHER,

You never lose sight of us.

No detail of our lives is hidden from Your sight. You see, and You act. You long for us to turn to You when we feel stressed. Share Your wisdom with us on how to relieve the pressure in our lives. Show us what changes we need to make in our schedules, our priorities, our methods of discipline, and our relationship with You. Then, pull us closer to You, like a loving Father cradling His troubled child.

Amen.

•   •   •

When

WE NEED TIME
TOGETHER . . .

Make the most of every opportunity.

COLOSSIANS 4:5

FATHER,

You long for our marriage to grow strong.

But, You know how difficult it is to take time for each other at this stage of our lives. When things get busy, prevent us from taking each other for granted. Help us do what we can to stay close physically and emotionally. Renew our commitment to growing closer to each other and You. We want to be a living, breathing picture of Your love. Teach us how to do that. Help us make the most of the moments we have.

Amen.

I am my lover's, the one he desires.

SONG OF SONGS 7:10 NLT

FATHER,

You created our desire for romance.

Thank You for making us for each other, for putting the longing in husbands and wives to want to spend time together. We need that time now. We need to relax in each other's arms and reconnect. Help us make that a reality. Time together always seems to fall to the bottom of the "To Do" list. We're tired, stressed, and all too often pinching pennies. Give us wisdom on how to "date" during this stage of our lives.

Amen.

Rejoice in the wife of your youth.

PROVERBS 5:18 NLT

FATHER,

You help us make the most of our time.

Don't let us neglect our relationship with each other when life gets hectic. Use us to refresh one another. Open our eyes to the opportunities that arise each day to spend time together in encouragement, companionship, and even romance. Please provide trustworthy babysitters to allow us to spend time away from our kids. Show us how to love one another deeply, creatively, and consistently. We don't want to settle for mediocrity in our marriage.

Amen.

> *Love never gives up, never loses faith, is always*
> *hopeful, and endures through every circumstance.*

1 CORINTHIANS 13:7 NLT

FATHER,

You are the Author of love.

You know what true love is, what it should look like in our lives. Reveal that to us. Show us how to serve and honor each other in the ordinary activities of each day. We need time alone, time to be lovers instead of parents. Help us find those moments. Help us set aside the distractions and frustrations of parenthood and get to know each other even better. Bless our marriage and let it be a blessing to our children.

Amen.

•   •   •

When

WE NEED TIME
WITH YOU . . .

I'm in the very presence of God—oh, how refreshing it is!

PSALM 73:28 THE MESSAGE

FATHER,

You complete us.

In Your presence is where we're most ourselves, so why do we put off spending time with You so frequently? We don't want to wait for that "quiet moment" that never comes. Show us how to spend time with You in prayer, praise, and learning from Your Word. Show us how to enjoy the pleasure of Your presence in the middle of cleaning the kitchen or running a carpool. Help us spend consistent time with You.

Amen.

Worship the Lord with the beauty of holy lives.

PSALM 96:9 TLB

FATHER,

You are holy.

You are worthy of our worship. Move us beyond the songs at church to worship You with our lives, not just our voices. Let everything we do today as parents be an offering that expresses our love for You. Meditating on Your gifts of love and forgiveness brings us to our knees. We are humbled by Your holiness. Fill our minds with thoughts of You. Lead us to Your throne throughout the day in worship, praise, and wonder.

Amen.

The grass withers, the flower fades, But the word of our God stands forever.

ISAIAH 40:8 NKJV

FATHER,

Your Word changes us.

Reading the Bible is unlike reading any other book. Forgive us for treating Your words like homework that we know we should do, but keep putting off. Make us thirsty for Your Scripture. We want to long for You, not just call on You whenever we need something. Help us make time to build a relationship with You that is more than just a passing acquaintance. Use Your Word to purify us, comfort us, refine us, and make us more like You.

Amen.

> *Each morning I will look to you in heaven and lay my requests before you, praying earnestly.*

PSALM 5:3 TLB

FATHER,

You wait for us.

You don't force yourself into our schedule. You don't show up unannounced and demand our attention. You wait patiently for us to come to You. That's what we want to do right now. Whisper words of love to our hearts every morning, so our day doesn't feel complete without drawing close to You. We give this day back to You. Show us how to use our time wisely and how to honor You with everything that lies before us.

Amen.

• • •

When

WE'RE FACING A
TRAGEDY . . .

FATHER,

You mourn with us.

Tragedy touches Your heart, as well as ours. Thank You for caring about the things that concern us, for not taking our human sorrow lightly. Our family needs Your comfort and strength. Let us know how near You are. Give us room to grieve and to heal. Show us how to share Your comfort with those around us. Help us be patient with ourselves and each other. Give us peace, in spite so many unanswered questions.

Amen.

> *You know that under pressure, your faith-life is forced into the open and shows its true colors.*

JAMES 1:3 THE MESSAGE

FATHER,

You help us grow.

Even through this, You're working. You're healing our hearts in ways we cannot fully understand. You're bringing comfort from unexpected directions. You're teaching us what faith looks like against the backdrop of an evil world. Let Your love shine through us during this time. Use us as Your arms to hold those who cannot stand alone. Use us to share Your words with those who are looking for answers. You are the only Answer we know. *Amen.*

•   •   •

When

WE FEEL
UNAPPRECIATED . . .

---

*Don't call attention to yourself; let others do
that for you.*

PROVERBS 27:2 THE MESSAGE

FATHER,

You see everything we do.

You know the ways we serve, the times we go beyond
what is necessary to do the very best job we can. It's hard
not to hear an audible "thank you" or "well done" along
the way. Who knows? Maybe that'll come someday. But,
please prevent our hearts from counting on it. Remind us
of why we're doing what we're doing. Help us persevere
out of love, not a desire to be honored. Make humility a
reality in our lives.

Amen.

> *"Let your good deeds shine out for all to see, so that everyone will praise your heavenly Father."*

MATTHEW 5:16 NLT

FATHER,

You are worthy of our praise.

When we do a good job, we want some of that praise to come our way, as well. When we hear criticism in its place, anger, resentment, bitterness, and defeat all battle to take root in our hearts. Don't let them, Lord. No matter what response we get from others, let love be our true motivation. Cleanse our prideful hearts. Use our hard work to draw attention to You and how You're working in our lives, instead of to ourselves.

Amen.

> *"If anyone wants to be first, he must be the very last, and the servant of all."*

MARK 9:35

FATHER,

You reward us.

You bless us in this life and the next. You take joy in watching us complete a job well done. Like any parent, You must feel proud when You see us maturing and sharing Your love. Let us find pleasure in Your pleasure in us. Parenting can feel like a thankless job. Please fill us with satisfaction and Godly pride in fulfilling the job of being the best parents we can be, regardless of how our kids respond.

Amen.

•   •   •

When

WE NEED WISDOM . . .

To learn, you must want to be taught.

PROVERBS 12:1 TLB

FATHER,

You value wisdom.

You honor wise people over fools. We want to be wise in Your eyes, not our own. Show us how to be parents who not only have knowledge about You, but also know You intimately. Make us eager pupils, willing to learn hard lessons about how to live a Godly life. Then, give us the courage to apply what we've learned. Make us wise parents who can impart wisdom to our kids through our words, actions, and prayers.

Amen.

In his heart a man plans his course, but the
LORD determines his steps.

FATHER,

You are greater than our plans.

We feel tugged in so many directions. Teach us to come to You first, not only before we set our own plans into action, but also before we even determine what those plans will be. Your wisdom is so much greater than our own. We need to lean on it, learn from it, and use it as our compass as we move forward. Thank You for Your desire to guide us toward what's best for our kids and us.

Amen.

Those who are wise will shine like the brightness of the heavens.

DANIEL 12:3

FATHER,

You lead us in love.

You never teach us by dragging us forward or letting us stumble around in the dark. You shine the light of Your wisdom on every step we take. You desire to make our hearts wise, like Yours. Expose the areas where we tend to be foolish. Show us how to encourage one another toward lives of integrity and good judgment. Help our decisions to not be based on emotion, popular opinion, or expediency, but on Your time-tested principles.

Amen.

A house is built by wisdom and becomes strong through good sense.

PROVERBS 24:3 NLT

FATHER,

You protect our family.

You guard us from our own selfishness and immaturity. The closer we get to You, the easier it is for us to tell the difference between wisdom and foolishness. Help us act on what You've taught us. It's so much easier for us just to act out of habit or emotion. We need Your wisdom in knowing the best way to discipline our kids, to teach them, and to love them. Help every decision we make be a sound one.

Amen.

*   *   *

When

WE ARE WORRIED . . .

God is greater than our worried hearts and knows more about us than we do ourselves.

---

1 JOHN 3:20 THE MESSAGE

FATHER,

You calm our worried hearts.

As we put each one of our fears into the palm of Your hand, we can see its true size in comparison to You. There's nothing You can't handle. And when You're the true Lord of our lives, there's nothing we can't handle because of our relationship with You. Give us perspective in this situation, Lord. We don't want to hold onto these fears any longer. Help us give each one of them to You right now.

Amen.

Surely, as I have planned, so it will be, and as I have purposed, so it will stand.

ISAIAH 14:24

FATHER,

You are in control.

Our hearts may not feel as though that's the truth, but it is. Every worry and anxious thought is just a reminder of how little control we have over our lives. Instead of panicking over our lack of control, help us rejoice in Your ultimate authority. You've proven Your love for us over and over. Nothing can happen that You haven't allowed or that You can't use for a positive purpose in our lives. Help us rest in that love and power.

Amen.

My God will meet all your needs according to his glorious riches.

PHILIPPIANS 4:19

FATHER,

You are rich in generosity.

You want to bless us and meet our needs. You long to fill our lives with joy. You desire to bring good out of evil. Help our hearts believe what our heads already know: that You want our best in this life. You never promised that life would be easy or without trouble, but You have promised that You are with us in it, supplying what we need when we need it to face whatever lies ahead. Thank You, Lord.

Amen.

Above all else, guard your heart, for it affects everything you do.

PROVERBS 4:23 NLT

FATHER,

You know our hearts are deceitful.

You know the lies that linger there, whispering worries to our weaknesses. Silence them with Your truth. Bring to mind verses of scripture that declare Your goodness and might. Replace our worries with praise and peace. Wipe away our doubts and fears. Guard us from anything or anyone that might draw us deeper into anxiety and distress, leading us away from the peaceful refuge of Your presence and promises.

Amen.

•　•　•

When

OUR CHILD IS AFRAID . . .

You are my hiding place; you will protect me from trouble and surround me with songs of deliverance.

PSALM 32:7

FATHER,

You are our child's hiding Place.

Better than hiding under the covers, our child can always hide in Your arms. Show us what we need to do to help lead him/her there. Release our child from irrational fears. Cover him/her with a sense of safety and rest. Quiet any anxious thoughts that are preventing our child from experiencing Your peace. Give us a sense of peace as well. Help us to rest in the knowledge that You are greater than our child's fears.

Amen.

The Lord is near.

PHILIPPIANS 4:5

FATHER,

You give us courage.

Just knowing who You are and how much You love us gives us the courage to face whatever is in our path. Help our child find that same courage. Be his/her Shield, high Tower, Protector, and Rescuer. Come to our child's rescue now. Whether in a tangible way or just by providing comfort and peace, take away our child's fears. Give us insight into what's real and what's just the product of an anxious heart.

Amen.

God has not given us a spirit of fear and timidity, but of power, love, and self-discipline.

2 TIMOTHY 1:7 NLT

FATHER,

You know our child's fears.

You know how strong of a hold they have on his/her heart. You know their source and power, and You also know what it will take to break their grip. Help our child break free from the fears that are holding him/her back from entering into Your joy and abundance. Show us what our part should be in this process. Quiet our own hearts, as well, and remind us that our child is never out of Your sight.

Amen.

I will fear no evil; For You are with me.

FATHER,

You are our Night-light in the darkness.

Even when life gets scary, You shine the light of reason on every situation. We know that fear often looms larger in the mind of a child than that of an adult. Help us be sensitive to that fact. Show us how to help our child find courage in the midst of his/her fear. Help our child move beyond his/her emotions toward Your truth. Encourage our child with the knowledge of Your presence and power.

Amen.

• • •

Everyday Prayers for Everyday Cares for Parents • 145

When

OUR CHILD FEELS ALONE . . .

You are safe in the care of the LORD your God, secure in his treasure pouch!

1 SAMUEL 25:29 NLT

FATHER,

You created us for relationship.

That's what our child's heart is longing for right now. Help fill that longing, not only with a deeper sense of Your love, but also with relationships that bring out the very best in him/her. Give our child the courage to reach out to others, to risk rejection by risking to love others. Show us how to provide comfort, companionship, understanding, and sacrificial love in a way that will teach our child how to give love and receive it.

Amen.

God sets the lonely in families.

PSALM 68:6

FATHER,

You made us a family.

You brought us together in Your wisdom and love. Help our child to feel at home in both our love and Yours. Replace his/her loneliness with a sense of belonging and contentment. Bring people into our child's life who will be faithful friends and positive influences in his/her life. Show us what we can do to help our child fit in and enjoy being the person You so lovingly created. Help our child find his/her place in this world.

Amen.

> *Even if my father and mother abandon me,*
> *the LORD will hold me close.*

PSALM 27:10 NLT

FATHER,

You hold our child close to Your heart.

Our child has never been alone and never will be; You're always right by his/her side. Even though we love our child more than we ever thought we could love anyone, we can't promise to always be there. But You can, You have, and You will. Our child needs a sense of Your presence right now. Help him/her to not feel so alone. Give our child a sense of being loved and accepted that goes deeper than words.

Amen.

• • •

When

OUR CHILD IS ANGRY . . .

"When someone gives you a hard time, respond with the energies of prayer, for then you are working out of your true selves, your God-created selves."

MATTHEW 5:44 THE MESSAGE

FATHER,

You help guard our emotions.

You help us respond, instead of react. You help us see beyond our child's angry words and actions, so we can understand why he/she is hurting or frustrated. Then, You provide wisdom to help us know how to deal with the real problem behind the anger. We ask that You would help us respond in love right now. Hold our emotions in check, and shield our hearts from being hurt by words our child really doesn't mean.

Amen.

Everyone should be quick to listen, slow to speak and slow to become angry.

JAMES 1:19

FATHER,

You know our child's heart.

You know where this anger is coming from. Give us insight into its cause. Help us discipline any words and actions that are inappropriate, but not overlook what's going on deeper inside. Help us get to the heart of our child's problem. We ask that You would give both us and our child wisdom to know why his/her emotions are so out of control. Please bring Your peace into our child's heart.

Amen.

When words are many, sin is not absent.

PROVERBS 10:19

FATHER,

You want our words to help, not hurt.

When our child is angry, it's so easy to let our own words get out of control. Stop the angry tirades going on in our own heads from making it to our lips. Give us wise words that will soothe our child and help him/her become more rational. Calm the emotions that keep bubbling to the surface. Bring our child to maturity in this area, and expose any problems we may have controlling our own anger as well.

Amen.

Look for the best in each other, and always do your best to bring it out.

1 THESSALONIANS 5:15 THE MESSAGE

FATHER,

You help us see the best in each other.

There's so much more to our child than his/her anger. There are so many things about our child that we love. Bring those things to mind right now. Show us how to bring out the best in our child, even when circumstances are difficult. Reveal to us any ways that we are being unfair or unloving. Show us anything that we are doing that could provoke our child to anger. Bring reconciliation, forgiveness, healing, and peace into our household. *Amen.*

•   •   •

When

OUR CHILD IS
DEPRESSED . . .

*As parents feel for their children, GOD feels
for those who fear him.*

PSALM 103:13 THE MESSAGE

FATHER,

You hurt for our child.

You made our child unique in all the world and in all
of time. You long for our child to understand how very
much he/she is loved by You and by us. Your desire is for
our child to celebrate life; to enjoy Your blessings; and to
learn how to love other people, as well as himself/herself.
Please bring these things to pass, Lord. Help our child
find joy in being the person You created him/her to be.

Amen.

Let our children see your glory at work.

FATHER,

Your hand is visible in this world.

From the beauty of a sunset to the birth of a child, Your creations testify to Your great glory and power. Even things we can't touch, like the gift of forgiveness or peace in the midst of pain, are evidence of Your love and involvement in our lives. Help our child see You and Your concern for him/her in the details of daily life. Make Your presence known in ways that will lift this depression from our child's heart.

Amen.

Encourage one another daily, as long as it is called Today.

FATHER,

Your love is deeper than our sorrow.

No matter how deep our child's depression, Your love for our child is deeper still. Thank You for touching his/her heart in places that we could never possibly reach. Your care for our child is a constant encouragement to us. Show us how to be an encouragement to him/her. Give us the wisdom to know what to say, what to do, and whom to turn to for help. Please wrap our child in answered prayers.

Amen.

Why am I discouraged? Why so sad? I will put my hope in God!

PSALM 42:5 NLT

FATHER,

You are the Healer of hearts.

You know what's causing this emotional pain in our child's life. We feel so confused and helpless; nothing we do or say seems to help. But You know our child better than we do. You know the source of this pain, as well as its cure. Lead us forward in wisdom. We long for our child to be free from this sadness and to experience Your gifts of joy, contentment, and purpose. Please remove whatever is blocking the way.

Amen.

•   •   •

When

OUR CHILD IS
DISAPPOINTED . . .

In perfect faithfulness you have done marvelous things, things planned long ago.

ISAIAH 25:1

FATHER,

You have done marvelous things.

You have fulfilled so many promises, answered so many prayers, and made so many dreams come true. But, our child can't see that right now. All our child can see is the disappointment that's looming larger than life right in front of him/her. Please open his/her eyes to the bigger picture. Help our child get beyond this setback. Meanwhile, help us to be patient in allowing our child the time he/she needs to mourn this loss.

Amen.

Pray in the Spirit on all occasions with all kinds of prayers and requests.

EPHESIANS 6:18

FATHER,

You lead us to prayer.

You've opened a way for us to speak to You, to Someone we can't even see or audibly hear. But, we know that You're listening, and we know that You move in our lives because of our conversations with You. We don't understand how it all works, but we know that it does. That's why we're turning to You now. Please help our child deal with this disappointment. Encourage our child in Your own unique way so that he/she won't lose heart. *Amen.*

> *As far as I am concerned, God turned into good what you meant for evil.*
>
> GENESIS 50:20 TLB

FATHER,

You don't waste our pain.

You turn our negative experiences into positive ones by stretching us in new directions and helping us grow. Please use this disappointment in our child's life in a positive way. Use it to draw him/her to You, not away from You. Soothe his/her hurt. Gently teach our child how his/her prayers are not always answered the way he/she pictures they will be. Help us learn that lesson as well.

Amen.

"Do not let your hearts be troubled. Trust in God."

JOHN 14:1

FATHER,

You never disappoint us.

Every promise You've made, You've kept. You surprise us with blessings and forgive us when it seems nearly impossible. You are worthy of our trust, our faith, and our adoration. As long as our child lives on this earth, he/she will know disappointment. No matter how much we long to shield our child from pain, we'll fail. But our child can trust in You without reservation. Help his/her faith in You grow through this disappointment.

Amen.

•   •   •

When

OUR CHILD NEEDS
DISCIPLINE . . .

Families stick together in all kinds of trouble.

PROVERBS 17:17 THE MESSAGE

FATHER,

You show us grace.

Help us to temper our discipline with grace as well.
Help us to set and enforce limits that allow for mistakes,
yet at the same time teach self-control and respect. Our
wisdom isn't sufficient to ensure that we'll always be fair
and loving parents. We need Your power and insight to
move beyond our own upbringings and inconsistent
emotions. Teach us forgiveness, grace, and patience as
our child matures.

Amen.

> *Discipline your children; you'll be glad you did—they'll turn out delightful to live with.*

PROVERBS 29:17 THE MESSAGE

FATHER,

You honor us with responsibility.

Our children are the most valuable, fragile gift You've ever given us. Our love and good intentions need Your strength and direction before they can result in consistent, effective parenting skills. We need Your help now as we face new challenges in dealing with our child's behavior. When nothing seems to work, lead us forward in hope and perseverance. Change our child's heart from the inside. Then, help us deal appropriately with what's occurring on the outside.

Amen.

Love is patient.

1 CORINTHIANS 13:4

FATHER,

You never lose control.

Unfortunately, the same can't be said for us. We know discipline should spring out of love, not anger. But, that's easier said than done. Help us mature in this area. Prepare our child's heart for the lessons that we need to teach him/her. Likewise, prepare our hearts for what You want to teach us through our child's behavior. Show us what we need to change to help our child overcome this problem. Expand our patience and bless our efforts.

Amen.

Be tender with sinners, but not soft on sin.

JUDE 1:23 THE MESSAGE

FATHER,

You hate sin.

But You love us. Even when we choose to go our own way, You never abandon us. Instead, You offer forgiveness, reconciliation, and growth. Help us offer those same things to our child. Show us how to help our child turn this area of his/her life around. Keep our child safe while he/she is struggling right now. Help us set fair boundaries and choose effective consequences for our child's actions. Lead our child to obedience.

Amen.

•   •   •

When

OUR CHILD IS DISRESPECTFUL . . .

Gentle words bring life and health.

PROVERBS 15:4 NLT

FATHER,

You know the power of words.

You know how they can build up relationships or tear them down. Our child's words are not only inappropriate, but they're also damaging hearts. Show us how to handle this problem without letting our own words get out of control. Help us to respond with love and wisdom. Please bring to the surface whatever is going on in our child's life that's causing this reaction to authority. Then, show us how to help him/her move beyond it.

Amen.

Let righteousness burst into blossom.

PSALM 72:7 THE MESSAGE

FATHER,

You desire righteousness.

You long for us to be conformed to Your character. We're a long way from that, Lord, and so is our child. He/She is fighting a battle that we're not sure how to handle. We can't demand respect. We can't force our child to regard us with honor. But we know that's the way You desire children to treat their parents. Make us worthy of that respect. Show us how to nurture an attitude of respect in our child.

Amen.

Do not follow the crowd in doing wrong.

EXODUS 23:2

FATHER,

You made us for relationship.

You've put a longing in us to feel like part of the group, to fit in. Our child longs for this just as we do, but we know that longing is only fulfilled by following Your design for our lives and by becoming who You've created us to be. We don't want to model our lives after anyone but You. Put this same desire in our child. Give him/her the courage to speak and act in a way that honors You.

Amen.

Sound leadership is founded on loving integrity.

PROVERBS 20:28 THE MESSAGE

FATHER,

You expose our pride.

Respect is something that we expect from our child. Our expectations aren't unreasonable or ungodly, but You know what's hidden behind those expectations. You know how easily our pride is hurt and how we get embarrassed when others see our child treating us with disrespect. Our desire for respect is born more out of self-ishness than a concern for our child's maturity. Deal with our pride. Then, give us wisdom to know how to deal with our child's insolence.

Amen.

•   •   •

When

OUR CHILD FAILS . . .

The wise person makes learning a joy.

PROVERBS 15:2 NLT

FATHER,

You help our child handle failure.

You don't make life failure-proof, but You do make it safe to turn to You in both failure and success. Our child is disappointed in himself/herself right now. Show us how to help our child learn from his/her mistakes. Give our child the strength to get up and try again. Help our home be a place where it's okay to not be perfect. Help us remember that we don't have to be perfect either.

Amen.

Fathers tell their children about your faithfulness.

ISAIAH 38:19

FATHER,

You ask us to be encouragers.

No matter how many times our child fails, help him/her understand that we don't love him/her any less. And neither do You. We need to know how to best communicate that to our child. Give us the opportunities, as well as the right words, to express how faithful You've been to our family. Help our child get to know You in a very personal way. Encourage him/her with a special sense of Your love during this tough time.

Amen.

• • •

When

OUR CHILD NEEDS FAITH . . .

You keep me going when times are tough—
my bedrock, GOD, since my childhood.

PSALM 71:5 THE MESSAGE

FATHER,

You are God.

How simple that sounds! But, so often we don't act as though it were true. Stretch our faith and make it grow. Then, do the same for our child. Let not just our words, but also our lives, be a consistent witness to Your sovereignty and faithfulness. Teach our family how to turn to You, not only when times are tough, but also throughout every ordinary, average day. Draw our child and us closer to Your side.

Amen.

Generation after generation stands in awe of your work; each one tells stories of your mighty acts.

PSALM 145:4 THE MESSAGE

FATHER,

Your mighty acts are recorded in the Bible.

Our child has heard stories of what You've done in the past. Please make these more than just fairy tales to him/her. Help our child understand that You're alive and active, that You're as involved in his/her life as You were in David's or Paul's or Mary's. Write new stories of Your power and majesty through our child's life. Put a hunger in our child's heart to find his/her place alongside You.

Amen.

You have been my God from the moment I was born.

PSALM 22:10 NLT

FATHER,

You've been calling to us since the day we were born.

We're not complete without You, and our hearts know it. Help our child recognize that what he/she is searching for can only be found in You. Bring people and circumstances into his/her life that will constantly point the way toward Your love and forgiveness. Help us allow our child the room he/she needs to grow in his/her own faith. Give us patience for this journey, and keep drawing us together in prayer.

Amen.

> *Point your kids in the right direction—when they're old they won't be lost.*

PROVERBS 22:6 THE MESSAGE

FATHER,

You encourage us as parents.

You never designed this job as one we should handle alone. You're always there leading us, strengthening us, protecting our kids, and replacing our discouragement with Your peace. Once again, we put our child in Your more than able hands. Hold him/her close. Bring things into our child's life that will cause his/her faith to grow. Replace his/her doubts with an assurance of Your loving presence. Shepherd our child to a place of spiritual maturity and abundance.

Amen.

•   •   •

When

OUR CHILD WANTS TO
GIVE UP . . .

> GOD *gives a hand to those down on their*
> *luck, gives a fresh start to those ready to quit.*
>
> PSALM 145:14 THE MESSAGE

FATHER,

You provide a fresh start.

You're the God of many chances. You never give up on us. Please help our child to not give up on himself/herself. Give him/her the strength to accept failure and learn from it. Give us compassion, and help us empathize with how our child is feeling right now. Help us understand why he/she feels so defeated. We need Your help to support our child in the way that reassures him/her of our love and acceptance.

Amen.

Well-done work has its own reward.

PROVERBS 12:14 THE MESSAGE

FATHER,

You understand discouragement.

You must experience it firsthand with every one of Your children, including every one of us in this family. So, You can understand the discouragement that our child is feeling right now, even if it is on a much smaller scale than Your own. Right now, our child seems to be filled with the desire to run away from this problem. Help him/her find a reason to continue to try.

Amen.

> *Let us run with perseverance the race marked out for us.*

HEBREWS 12:1

FATHER,

You want us to persevere.

First, we need to make sure that we're running in the right direction. Which direction is our child going? We need wisdom in discerning when it's appropriate for our child to quit and when he/she needs to keep trying. Help us see what's best for him/her, not just for us. We long to come alongside our child and cheer him/her on to success in whatever he/she wants to do. What direction do You want our child to go?

Amen.

> Be brave. Be strong. Don't give up. Expect
> GOD to get here soon.

PSALM 31:24 THE MESSAGE

FATHER,

You will never desert our child.

You'll never let him/her face a challenge alone. Come to his/her rescue right now. Help our child understand his/her own strengths and weaknesses and how You can use both to bring about wonderful things. Show yourself as a faithful Father and Friend. Answer our child's prayers in the way that he/she will best understand that You are at work in his/her life. Lord, please do the same for us as well.

Amen.

•   •   •

When

OUR CHILD IS
GRIEVING . . .

When you pass through the waters, I will be with you.

ISAIAH 43:2

FATHER,

You are never surprised by what happens.

But we are. We know that You love us and answer prayer, but it's hard to hold onto those truths in light of these circumstances. If it's hard for us, we know it's even harder for our child. Please comfort his/her heart with a peace that makes no sense in light of all that's happened—a peace that could only come from You. Show us how to help our child share his/her heart with us. Help us heal together.

Amen.

> *"You're blessed when the tears flow freely. Joy comes with the morning."*

LUKE 6:21 THE MESSAGE

FATHER,

You created our tears.

You knew we'd need them, that somehow they'd help us heal. Even Your Son cried when He was on this earth. Please help our child cry healing tears. Then dry them from within with Your gentle hand. Give us wisdom in answering our child's questions and the humility to say, "we don't know" when we don't. Teach us how to be Your arms of comfort for our child, to help him/her grieve and heal.

Amen.

•   •   •

When

OUR CHILD IS ILL . . .

I am a man of prayer.

PSALM 109:4

FATHER,

You have the power to heal.

We're asking You to use that power now. We know You have plans that often differ from our own, but You've also asked us to pray about everything, to bring all of our requests to You. That's what we're doing now. We long for our child to feel whole and healthy. Please give us wisdom to know what we can do to help. We're placing our most precious treasure in Your healing hands. We trust in Your love and power.

Amen.

> *Make our sons in their prime like sturdy oak trees, Our daughters as shapely and bright as fields of wildflowers.*

PSALM 144:12 THE MESSAGE

FATHER,

You love our child.

You know his/her body intimately. You know what needs to be done to bring healing. Would You please bring that healing, whether it's through a miracle, medicine, or simply the passage of time? Give our child relief from his/her discomfort and fears. We know that You're right there by our child's side, through every waking and sleeping moment. Please comfort him/her with a sense of Your presence and peace. Comfort our own anxious hearts as well.

Amen.

•   •   •

When

OUR CHILD NEEDS PROTECTION . . .

The LORD protects me from danger—so why should I tremble?

PSALM 27:1 NLT

FATHER,

You protect us.

You do not sit idly by when we're in danger. You're active and involved, leading, guiding, protecting, and participating in our lives. Protect our child now. Guard him/her physically, emotionally, mentally, and spiritually. Help us rest in the knowledge that You love our child even more than we do. Take away our fears. Replace them with a diligence in prayer and wisdom in knowing what action we need to take. Help us to remember that You are our Peace.

Amen.

He who watches over you will not slumber.

PSALM 121:3

FATHER,

You never sleep.

You know how sleepless our nights are when we're worried about our child, but worries never keep You awake. Your love for us is what keeps You ever-watchful, ever-present. We know that You are with our child right now. Take these prayers and use them in Your own mysterious ways to surround our child with Your protection. Be his/her safe House. Bring help from unexpected people and places. Quiet our hearts, as we give You each one of our fears.

Amen.

Is any one of you in trouble? He should pray.

FATHER,

You listen.

You hear every word our anxious hearts speak. You even hear our sighs and groans, and You understand the prayers behind them that go deeper than words. Listen to those prayers now. Come to our child's rescue. Keep him/her safe. Guard those around him/her as well. Bless our child with wisdom and discernment that reaches beyond his/her years. Lead our child safely down the path that You've set before him/her today.

Amen.

•   •   •

When
Our Child Is
Rebellious . . .

Forgive the rebellious sins of my youth.

Psalm 25:7 NLT

Father,

Your love gives us hope.

You never let Your children go. You pursue them with love and tenacity, for a lifetime if necessary. Thank You for pursuing each of us and for the mercy and forgiveness You've shown. Our child needs You now. We'll never stop loving him/her, but we're at a loss as to what to do. Don't let this rebelliousness consume all of our time and energy. Help us do what we can and leave the rest in Your hands.

Amen.

The LORD will fight for you; you need only to be still.

EXODUS 14:14

FATHER,

You will fight for our child.

There's a battle going on for his/her heart. Nobody understands that as well as You do, but some days it feels as though the battle is already lost. We're fighting our own battle with fear, discouragement, and disappointment. We desperately need Your strength and perspective. Work in our lives and in the life of our child. Draw us together as a family so that we can help our child move past rebellion to repentance.

Amen.

> *Young people are prone to foolishness and fads;*
> *the cure comes through tough-minded discipline.*

PROVERBS 22:15 THE MESSAGE

FATHER,

You let us choose our own paths.

You never force us to follow You. You simply continue to draw us to yourself with Your love. But right now, we're afraid of the path our child is choosing to follow. We can set limits, give advice, and pray; but only You can change our child's heart and direction. That's our heartfelt prayer. Let Your truth shine brighter than all of the enticing lies that are surrounding our child right now. Keep calling out to his/her heart.

Amen.

Every living soul belongs to me.

EZEKIEL 18:4

FATHER,

You know the pain of rebellion.

Your children have turned against You since the dawn of time. You know how our child's attitude and actions break our hearts, and we know how they break Yours as well. Please turn our pain into prayers instead of anger, bitterness, or despair. Help us move past our own feelings of hurt and failure to learn what unconditional love looks like—a love that keeps giving even in the face of rejection. Thank You that we don't have to face this alone.

Amen.

•   •   •

When

OUR CHILD NEEDS
WISDOM . . .

> *To discipline and reprimand a child pro-duces wisdom.*
>
> PROVERBS 29:15 NLT

FATHER,

You use us to impart wisdom.

But we cannot share what we do not have. Increase our wisdom by never letting our relationship with You grow stagnant. Stretch us, refine us, cleanse us, and use us greatly in our child's life. Show us now how to help our child grow in wisdom and discernment. We ask that You would not only help him/her grow in knowledge and common sense, but that You would also help him/her know how to apply these traits to real life.

Amen.

Wisdom is found in those who take advice.

PROVERBS 13:10

FATHER,

You created us to help one another.

You made each of us unique, with different strengths and weaknesses. Use our strengths now to help our child in his/her areas of weakness. Give us wise words, and even more importantly, help us to live Godly lives. Surround our child with friends and mentors whose wisdom comes from You. Soften our child's heart toward the words he/she hears. Help him/her be open to advice and correction. Build wisdom into every area of his/her life.

Amen.

Additional copies of this book and other
titles from Honor Books
are available from your local bookstore.

Everyday Prayers for Everyday Cares
Everyday Prayers for Everyday Cares for Women
Everyday Prayers for Everyday Cares for Mothers

If you have enjoyed this book,
or if it has impacted your life,
we would like to hear from you.

Please contact us at:

Honor Books

Department E

P.O. Box 55388

Tulsa, Oklahoma 74155

Or by e-mail at *info@honorbooks.com*

—